I am Keats

Also by Tom Asacker

Sandbox Wisdom
The Four Sides of Sandbox Wisdom
A Clear Eye for Branding
A Little Less Conversation
Opportunity Screams
The Business of Belief

I am Keats

Escape Your Mind and Free Your Self*

Tom Asacker

*It's not what you think

Portions of this book have appeared in somewhat different form on the author's website.

Printed in the United States of America

ISBN-10: 1540724999
ISBN-13: 978-1540724991

First Edition: 2017

Library of Congress Cataloguing in Publication Data: A catalog record for this book is available from the Library of Congress

Cover design by T.E.A.

To our older selves

Contents

I don't know where I'm going from here, but I promise it won't be boring.

— David Bowie

Introduction

We are all living in cages with the door wide open.

— George Lucas

Lock and Key

Budapest-born Erik Weisz was one of seven children.

He arrived in the United States in his mother's arms in 1878.

Twenty-two years later Harry Handcuff Houdini was baffling police in Scotland Yard.

He had let go of what he was and became the world's most famous escape artist.

Houdini boasted he could break out of any jail cell in the world in less than one hour.

And every time he was tested he would escape in just a few short minutes.

But one time things didn't go as Houdini had planned.

As the story goes, a small town in the British Isles built a new lockup.

And they haughtily invited Houdini to come give their showpiece a try.

As usual Houdini accepted the challenge without hesitation.

He arrived and strolled into the cell pregnant with confidence.

And once the door was closed and he was left alone, Houdini went to work.

He coughed up a special lock pick, quickly released his handcuffs and homed in on the door.

But there was something strange about this particular lock.

Thirty tortuous minutes dragged on and Houdini was rattled.

After sixty, Houdini was crestfallen and drenched in sweat.

Exhausted, he collapsed against the heavy metal door.

And it swung open.

Houdini was astonished to discover that the door was never locked.

At least not in objective reality.

It was only locked in his mind.

There's a quote often attributed to the great Houdini:

"My mind is the key that sets me free."

Minds can certainly be keys.

But more often they are locks.

The Lock

You and I are like Houdini.

We're confined in mental prisons of our own creation and the locks to those cells are the stories we tell ourselves, stories that are "make-believe." We make them up—or others make them up for us—and eventually we come to believe them.

We call those inherited and learned accounts of life, "reality."

Do you feel held back by your reality, by the stories you're telling yourself about yourself and your life?

I've been smothered by mine on more than a few occasions, locked up in a stifling cell of my own creation. So far I've managed to find a way out and, thankfully, it was never a Houdini-like, public spectacle.

During my most recent lock down, around three years ago, I felt like a caged animal. I found myself pacing back and forth, seriously stuck, and I had no idea where to turn or what to do.

There, I've said it.

You wouldn't have noticed; no one did. But it came over me like a dark cloud.

I don't think it was depression; I didn't feel sad or worthless. I felt spiritless and confused. I'd spent a lifetime studying psychology, philosophy, mythology, brain science, human decision-making, blah, blah, blah, and I could not make a *meaningful* decision to save my life.

The Incite

That's not hyperbole. I was living but I wasn't alive, and it was killing me. Surprisingly, the malignant "it" strangling me was my own cleverly constructed story, my own mind. Knowledge—or the illusion of knowledge—was suffocating me in a fictitious box of my own making.

I'd heard about, read about, and experienced so much that I was sure that I could predict the future, except stock prices and lottery numbers.

And since I knew what was going to happen before I even tried, why bother in the first place? Rumination was slowly seducing me to consume myself, like *Ouroboros* devouring its own tail.

And then, on a whim, I had breakfast with a friend.

After bringing each other up to date and eventually ordering our food, the conversation turned to parenthood and his oldest son who was similarly stuck. The twenty-something was living at home, unhappy, but "so damn smart that it's impossible to reason with him."

As I reached for my bottomless cup of coffee, I remember thinking, "Hmm, sounds familiar. Now, if we could only wipe his memory clean, he'd be easy to reason with and we could guide him, get him moving again." And for some unknown reason that idea grabbed hold of my imagination, and it would not let go.

I walked out of the restaurant that fateful day and spontaneously spun that "aha" moment into a high-concept idea for a movie. And that set me off on a screenwriting adventure where, as

William James so aptly described the creative process, I was "suddenly introduced into a seething cauldron of ideas, where everything is fizzling and bobbing about in a state of bewildering activity."

And from that stirring state of wonder, all kinds of feelings, thoughts, metaphors and philosophies mysteriously emerged. Ideas that were so compelling—and which resonated so deeply with everyone I shared them with—that I was moved to write this book, and to create an online platform to help others assimilate the concepts and practices.

The New Scene

But as I sit here now, reflecting on that day, I'm honestly not sure how events unfolded. Did I come up with an idea for a movie based on that conversation over blueberry pancakes? Were we even eating breakfast, or was it lunch at that Indian joint? Maybe the idea was simmering in my mind prior to our conversation and his story simply turned up the heat.

I know I'll eventually come up with an idiosyncratic story to tell—one that makes sense to me and resonates with others—because, after all, that's what human beings do; we conjure up and tell stories.

And I also know that my new scene, like the one that was holding me back, will end up moving me forward into a new future.

This is not a revelation to me. I've known the power that people's invented stories wield over their decisions and success for a long time. In fact, I wrote a book about it and gave a popular TEDx talk where I confidently proclaimed:

"We embody our roles, our values, our stories. We live in those stories, and we live according to them."

Serendipity

But here's the thing:

I didn't appreciate the stifling dimension of those words, especially on my own life, until quite recently. And I certainly had no idea that the impulsive decision and spontaneous process of writing a screenplay would make it viscerally clear, and eventually change the way I look at and live my life.

Imagine, here I was thinking that I was informing my work, when all along my work was informing me.

The unfamiliar structure and process of film storytelling, the characters and scenes, the fortuitous encounters and peculiar insights, all revealed powerful parallels to living an authentic and passionate life, many of which were hidden from me.

Life is full of paradoxes like that and, in the chapters that follow, you will be introduced to others that emerged during the creation of the screenplay, *I am Keats*. I refer to them as "secrets" because no one ever told me about them. They were, oddly, unforeseen.

"Oddly," because remember, I thought I knew everything.

Secrets Revealed

Before I reveal them to you let me make a few things clear, which may help curb one-star reviews frantically composed by readers who were looking for a step-by-step recipe or formula.

First, these "secrets to success" are not surefire strategies to help you "hack" your present life, making you wealthier or more productive.

It may happen, but frankly I couldn't care less.

More importantly, they're not a quick fix. There are no techniques or how-tos that you can easily absorb and rapidly put into action. To the contrary, what I'm about to tell you will appear quite strange at first. They're simple ideas but they're unfamiliar and unfashionable, and that's the difficulty of understanding them.

Paradoxically simple things can often be the most difficult, as you will soon discover.

Rather, these secrets are new ways of thinking to help you slowly and surely break out of your personal mental prison and enlarge your sense of possibility.

But as you read on, you may find yourself becoming skeptical and wondering, "What does he mean by that? Where is this thing going? What am I supposed to do with this?"

Trust me, I get it. You're looking for structure, a narrative. And that's one way to approach this type of book: to expound a theory and then break it down and rearrange it into a logical framework, using examples as proof.

The other way is to use various examples, metaphorically and illustratively, to convey the truth directly to your inner voice, to your gut. I have chosen this second approach, and through it I hope to enable you to enter the complex, inner workings of your own mind by the back door so to speak.

So relax and just let go. I'm not trying to sell you on these ideas or convert you to anything. I'm asking you to play with the concepts. If you don't feel like you're stuck in your own story, then for heaven's sake don't waste your time with this book. There's plenty to watch on Netflix.

On the other hand if you do feel a bit lost or boxed in, like life is uninspired and tedious, then it's time to break your addiction to comfort and embrace the greatest paradox of all:

When you're stuck between a rock and a hard place you must use the *rock* to breakthrough the hard place. You have to use your mind to escape your mind and free your self.

It's one heady trip (pun intended), and it's not a journey for the faint-hearted. I continue to struggle to put these concepts into practice. But, as you'll soon discover, there is nothing more liberating or satisfying. Because when you finally find the courage to embrace life's paradoxes and choose your own journey, life will find a way to embrace you right back.

And who knows? It may even rock your world.

It certainly rocked mine.

One

The blizzard of the world has crossed the threshold and it has overturned the order of the soul.

— Leonard Cohen

A Little Less Coleridge

The Romantic poet John Keats lived his short life with intense passion.
Moved by his senses and imagination.
He longed to find beauty in a world of suffering.
And his writing is a radiant reflection of those dreams.
Keats was also a great admirer of Shakespeare.
He once described the Bard's genius as Negative Capability:

"At once it struck me, what quality went to form a Man of Achievement, especially in literature, and which Shakespeare possessed so enormously. I mean Negative Capability, that is when man is capable of being in uncertainties, mysteries, doubts, without any irritable reaching after fact and reason."

Uninhibited, open, without judgment.
Giving oneself fully to the process, to that which is being experienced.
Without the need to figure it all out, or the desire for gain.
Sadly, that sentiment is antithetical to today's goal-obsessed culture.
An anxiety-fueled zeitgeist that is sucking the spirit out of people.
And which, I'm pretty sure, was the crux of my angst.
For I often found myself wondering.
Why do it? What's its purpose? What's it going to accomplish?
Driven, instinctively, by my insatiable desire to understand, to connect the dots.
Just like another Romantic poet, Samuel Taylor Coleridge.

Who obsessively searched for "the truth" of the human condition.
And the mysteries of the natural world.
Keats saw Coleridge's compulsion as narrowly subjective.
Keats believed that the inspirational power of beauty was more important than the quest for meaning.
It has taken me quite a while to wake up to it, assuming I actually have.
But Keats was right.
In our dogged pursuit of knowledge and goals, we have forgotten to live.
To subdue self-concern and identify with others.
To open up fully to here-and-now experiences.
And to embrace our empathetic impulses and imaginative creativity.
So I'm going to try to stop connecting all of the dots.
It's really hard.
Stop trying to predict an unknowable future.
Even harder.

And instead, be a connected and passionate part of the present.
For as Goethe made clear, "What is important in life is life, and not the result of life."
Here's to life!
A little less Coleridge.
A lot more Keats.

Two Minds

Keats wrote, "What the imagination seizes as beauty must be the truth." And Coleridge proclaimed, "Nothing is so contagious as enthusiasm."

Truth and enthusiasm.

When you approach life in that order, when you lead with your inner truth and stoke those instincts with resolve, success is inevitable. Unfortunately that's not how we've been conditioned to think and behave, and it took a bunch of characters in a fictional story to make that clear to me.

I almost didn't discover that underlying insight, which I'll explore throughout the book, because my "Coleridge-mind" was not enthusiastic.

It kept prodding:

"Why are you writing a *screenplay*? Who are *you* to write a screenplay? Do you know how many *people* are writing screenplays? What does a successful screenplay *sell* for, anyway?"

"Is the juice worth the squeeze?"

It's strange, I know, but at some point during my unexpected new scene I began referring to my two minds, or two of my minds, as Keats and Coleridge. It is now part of my conceptual system, influencing how I perceive, how I think, and what I do. It's a powerful mental construct and metaphor, which I call upon daily to help me interpret and guide various feelings and decisions.

How did this happen? I honestly can't remember and it really doesn't matter. What matters is what those two minds have come to represent. And in case you're unaware, we are definitely of, at least, two minds.

I happen to side with Walt Whitman:

"Do I contradict myself? Very well then I contradict myself, (I am large, I contain multitudes.)" But for now, let's stick with the two.

Feeling and Thinking

Plato imagined a chariot being pulled by two horses. The charioteer is the rational part of the mind that is trying to guide the more impulsive passions; one principled and the other amoral.

The social psychologist Jonathan Haidt uses the metaphor of a rider—the conscious, reasoning mind—on the back of an elephant—the more powerful and automatic, implicit mind.

There's also the left brain / right brain theory, which has recently been debunked. The two systems of cognitive processes described by behavioral economist Daniel Kahneman, which is presently under scrutiny. And who can possibly forget Nietzsche's philosophical dichotomy, Apollonian and Dionysian, or Freud's id and ego?

I'll tell you who. Me, that's who.

In fact, no theory of mind or metaphor has stuck with me long enough to help me make decisions that serve both my short and long-term desires.

But then, while writing about the two main characters in the screenplay *I am Keats*, I happened upon the 19th century English Romantic poets John Keats and Samuel Taylor Coleridge.

Keats and Coleridge had distinctly different predispositions towards life. Keats was attracted to the real and tangible; the sensuous sights and sounds of nature, as well as the joys and suffering of mankind.

Coleridge was driven more by thoughts and reflections, philosophical musing and intellectual abstraction; the representative and instructive nature of the world.

This is a Metaphor

I am not an authority on 19th century Romantic poets, and this is certainly a sweeping generalization, so please view it purely as an ontological metaphor; a model of the mind.

For the time being let Keats represent your *feeling* mind, "the order of the soul"—imagination, spontaneity, uncertainty, experience—and

Coleridge your *thinking* mind, "the blizzard of the world"—logic, order, control, progress.

Now, I can assure you that the blizzard of Coleridge has you pinned to the ground, otherwise you wouldn't be reading this book.

Coleridge wants to take care of you, to make sure that you live a productive and mistake-free life. When he's sure you're under control, he'll let you up, brush you off and help you plan, analyze, and keep score. He'll (mis)guide you on a calculated and relatively comfortable journey.

"But," you may be thinking, "that doesn't make sense. If Coleridge is holding me down, that must mean *he's* more powerful than Keats. But aren't Plato's winged, muscular horses and Haidt's massive elephant representative of the *feeling* mind? And if so, then isn't *Keats* more powerful and, therefore, in control?"

You've arrived at another paradox, at least given commonly accepted theories of mind, which suggest that the heart and the head are divided.

The proposition becomes more clear when you realize that Keats is not an impulsive child, nor a mindless beast reacting to stimuli and jumping to conclusions like a dog on a leash. Keats is an *informed* state of mind, as much cognitive as emotional. He is acutely aware of what he's doing, and of why he's doing it.

And for that matter, so is Coleridge.

The Designer and the Engineer

The state of mind with the most influence over your life is the one in charge of your intentions.

Keats's intention is to create and to share, to live a life brimming with passion, exploration and affection. Think of Keats as your life designer. He's an artist, turned on by emotive desire. Like a wide-eyed child, he's pulled by curiosity and schooled by discomfort and failure.

Keats looks at the world of infinite possibility and wonders, "Why the hell not?"

Coleridge's goal, on the other hand, is to make everything predictable and stable. Coleridge is your life engineer. He's an expert craftsman, skilled in the rights and wrongs of the world, and turned on by the desire for risk aversion, accumulation and conformity. Like a paranoid helicopter parent, he wants everything to be safe, productive, and acceptable.

Coleridge looks at every situation and thinks, "But what will happen if?"

To live a successful life we need to be conscious, or meta-aware, of the working relationship between Keats and Coleridge. We have to wake up and listen, without judgment, to the constant poetic struggle going on between our ears.

The Scottish philosopher David Hume postulated that, "Reason is, and ought only to be the slave of the passions." He even went so far as to call reason impotent.

I happen to agree with Hume's preference but, unfortunately, reasoning Coleridge isn't a slave. He has his own desires and he *will* tap into Keats' feelings and make him *his* slave, if you let him.

You're probably well aware of Coleridge's desires, how he measures success and what he considers a good life. It's been drilled into you since you were a child. In fact, it's so pervasive and entrenched in our society that Merriam Webster's online dictionary lists it as the very first definition of success:

"The fact of getting or achieving wealth, respect, or fame."

Negative Capability

Wealth, respect, and fame: three positive goals that lead to success. Positive, because the goal is to get or achieve *more*. In fact, the more the better. At least that's what we've been led to believe.

But what if the achievement of true success emerges by subtraction? What if the secret to living a meaningful, vibrant, and rewarding life requires us to pursue a *negative* goal?

That's negative capability: to negate the self-concerned, conditioned, thinking mind. It's not something that you do or achieve. It's something that you *undo*. You unwind your conscious mind, suspend the act of comparison, and relax into a state of acceptance, unselfconsciousness and receptivity. It is a daunting and relentless task, because we're wired to strive and compare, to look ahead and figure things out.

It's probably why our bloodline survived while our more Keatsian ancestors met their demise. They were smelling roses while our ancestral progenitors were busy sharpening stones and hoarding food.

But that was then, and this is now.

To obsessively plan and calculate in today's modern, connected world is to lock yourself away in an instrumental prison, sheltered from the vibrancy of life. Instead, you must let go of your incessant desire to know, to predict and to influence, and instead be willing to experience the mystery of the present without corrupting it with questions.

Of course, you will never master negative capability, just as Zen monks never master enlightenment. Why they're called Zen "masters" is another mystery. Rather it is something you *practice;* a new way of being that will slowly shift the way you perceive the world and experience life. One that will help you distinguish the voices in your head, and which will progressively reveal internal insights that move you to embrace your truest self and create something unique and inspiring.

Two

The most courageous act is still to think for yourself. Aloud.

— Coco Chanel

You are Your Warden

Young Galileo Galilei wanted to be a priest.
His musician father pushed him to study medicine.
But at University Galileo was serendipitously turned on by mathematics and physics.
Particularly ideas about objects in motion.
Five decades later Galileo's desire-driven thinking rocked people's world.
He wrote, "Thought is the most pleasing ability granted to humankind."
And for bringing the gifts of his passionate inner world to the external world?
Galileo was imprisoned.
Because his dynamic thinking challenged the static thinking of the established order.

A world that saw itself as the center of the universe.
It was heresy to advocate Copernican heliocentrism.
The idea that the Earth travels around the Sun.
And to suggest that Aristotle's perfect Sun had spots?
The Roman Catholic Church would have none of it!
So Galileo was forced to "abjure, curse and detest" his beliefs.
And spend the final nine years of his life under house arrest.
Mathematician, physicist, astronomer, inventor, and philosopher.
Einstein called Galileo the father of modern science.
But he was much more than that.
Galileo was the courageous father of freethinking.
A fountainhead whose spirited story awakened the earth.
And inspired the masses to think as well.

But here's the thing.

Galileo's passionate ordeal made something quite clear.

Thinking is not an objective, open-minded process.

Like discerning the movement of planets.

If it were we'd simply evaluate data, weigh the evidence, and make rational decisions.

Ones based on the "facts."

But life is not a fact-based, objective reality.

It's a truth-based, subjective construct.

One colored by an aggregation of personal experiences.

And interpreted through an ever shifting perceptual lens.

Your mind, my mind, everyone's mind is like the Catholic Church.

It is steeped in history and resistant to change.

Especially change that threatens its established order.

Its made-up story!

Its unique perceptions, beliefs and identity formed over a lifetime of devotion.

This established order of the mind acts like a director working behind the scenes.
To keep us at the center of things.
To make sure that our world remains consistent and coherent.
And to guarantee that we follow our "script."
So yes, Galileo helped us see that humans aren't the center of the physical universe.
But make no mistake.
We are the center of our personal universe.
Whether we're conscious of it or not.
And, like the church with Galileo, that self-involved and self-protective view of your world is what's keeping us and our future under house arrest.
You are your warden.
So am I.

Life is Not a Story

So what will happen if you break free? What unique and inspiring phenomenon will emerge if you get control over *your* director, over Coleridge?

I hesitate to answer, since it plays right into Coleridge's hands.

Do you see the paradox? Coleridge will let Keats lead, but only if Keats can assure him that the story will turn out fine and the outcome will be worth the effort.

I struggled mightily with that tension. My passion was almost derailed on many occasions by those self-concerned reflections; thoughts about my present "circumstances."

Circumstances are the particular compulsion of Coleridge. He's obsessed with what you're doing and why. He wants you to stay in role, follow your script and to be productive, in order to *build up* your self-esteem and to *store up* for those imagined times ahead.

If you look up the word "circumstance" in a thesaurus one particular word is referenced that is highly pertinent to this ethos: "scene."

I don't know about you, but when I was young my parents taught me to *never* make a scene:

"Tommy! Knock it off, you're making a scene!"

Based on my new way of looking at life, that was terrible advice. And it wasn't really "advice." Scenes are what make your life exciting and memorable, especially when they break from your invented story. In fact, every single successful experience in my life emerged because I liberated my spirit and created a scene, or else I jumped into one.

Do you realize that your life is comprised of a bunch of random scenes? I didn't. Sure, I knew that I made up a story in my head about my life. In fact, I wrote all about it in my previous book on belief.

Knowing vs. Being

But there's a world of difference between *knowing* that humans think in narratives to form beliefs and make sense of their lives, and seeing through that illusion to *feel* that one's life *isn't* a story; it's a bunch of unplanned, hit-or-miss events.

It's like the difference between *knowing* what love is and *being* madly in love.

Knowing is a safe, intellectual construct of words and fantasies. *Being* is a frightening awareness, a dynamic dance with reality. Frightening, because it's complex and demanding, and you have no idea where it may take you.

It's strange, I've written six books but I was not prepared for where the screenplay adventure was taking me. Strange, chance encounters with people and ideas spoke directly to me. Some were mere whispers, while others were deafeningly loud and crystal clear. And they were all saying the same thing:

"Stop thinking! Let life tell you what *it* wants you to do."

I'm not used to that kind of advice. I'm impatient, a consummate seeker, and one of the world's greatest skeptics. My university degree is in economics, after all; the dismal science, but a science nonetheless.

But try as I may, and I really tried, I could not make sense of those "voices." I knew full well that human beings find what they are looking for, that we're hardwired to seek patterns and connect the dots, but the messages were so startlingly specific that I could not fathom how my mind was making meaning.

I ultimately figured that I could do one of two things: accumulate more information to help me rationalize the idea, or simply let go and see what happens.

Believe or have faith.

I wrote a book about belief, but I had absolutely no understanding of the profound difference between those two concepts.

Belief vs. Faith

Belief is how we make most of life's decisions.

Belief is like crossing a footbridge stretched above a deep chasm. Our desire for what's on the other side—our goal or vision of the future—is what gets us on the path. And evidence that the bridge is safe and that we're making progress towards that goal is what keeps us walking across.

Beliefs touch every facet of our lives, mundane and profound, from the religions we choose to inform our spiritual and moral lives to the products we purchase to make us look "hot."

Belief is a comforting conviction *and* a self-fulfilling prophecy. And that's why we typically restrict ourselves to only desiring what we are confident we can obtain, based on our story.

Faith, on the other hand, requires neither a clear vision nor confirming evidence, not even a bridge. All faith requires is a *feeling* of truth, an intellectual instinct. And then it's a running leap across the chasm and into the unknown.

Faith gets you airborne, where everything looks strange and feels frightening.

And it keeps you there, floating in uncertainty. And that's why passionate love, great art, breakthrough ideas and the creative, uncompromising execution of bold visions are hard, and noticeably scarce.

You're Not in Control

There was no way I could accumulate enough evidence to "believe," to feel assured. Yes, I read all "the books" and online "advice." I also studied and analyzed the "best" screenplays and even consulted "the experts." And what I discovered was a bottomless pit of conflicting information about everything and everyone, and it was constantly changing.

It quickly became apparent to me that my *knowing* would never create the *doing*.

That said, I didn't wing it. I'm well aware that skill and discipline are necessary for creative expression. But I also realized that my invisible idea was really about me and my new scene. It was a mysterious force trying to claw its way out of my chest. All I had to do was close my eyes, unlock my heart, let it out and see what happens.

The doing would have to create the knowing.

And what happens when you let go and let it out, when you're possessed like I was with an idea, in this case, with a movie? The same thing that happens when you finally let go and live. Your intuitive intelligence wakes up and starts moving you along a strange journey of discovery and creation.

You find yourself being pulled deeper and deeper into a process that creates serendipitous connections and refines your perceptions. Your old eyes adjust to a new world, and you become more creative *and* discerning.

Moved by Keats

I've experienced that awesome feeling in various scenes during my life.

As a practicing magician I was suddenly able to redirect people's attention, sober people, without even trying, like they were hypnotized. In art class, my eyes unexpectedly woke up and I started seeing solid colors as an amazing composite of hues.

While deep into the process of running a medical device company, a chance encounter with a child's toy triggered a breakthrough, patentable idea. It also happened to me practicing martial arts, playing various sports, consulting with clients, and while writing three of my six books.

Sadly, my other three books were goal-driven. Coleridge took the lead and viewed them as a means to an end, that end being those aforementioned measures of success. They weren't birthed and nurtured by Keats—that mysterious, internal force—and it showed.

It's difficult for me to describe my screenwriting experience, because it sounds kind of new-agey. It felt like what I was doing was actually doing me, almost like a dream. I honestly didn't know where the ideas were coming from. It was truly, very strange.

Characters simply appeared. Scenes arose spontaneously, magically pouring out of me and my writing partner, Shannon. And as its vessel, its agent, I felt my job was, pretty much, *not* to screw it up; to nurture the organic, evolving story without killing it with my impatient, controlling mind (otherwise known as negative capability).

Be Quiet and Listen

One of the most powerful secrets I discovered while letting it have its way with me is that dancing with those feelings is the same challenge you have with your unfolding life. Your inner spirit, your unique brilliance, *wants* to get out, but in its own way and at its own pace.

Keats wants to celebrate your individuality, to move you to make a scene, to try new things and to experience love, beauty and enthusiasm. But you have to stop doubting, listen, and be unconditionally receptive to its calling. Make no mistake:

It is really hard to do.

Someone wrote that the easiest thing to be in the world is you. That someone was wrong.

Your Calling

And here's another powerful secret that revealed itself to me:

A "calling" is not a life purpose. It's a voice whispering in your ear, *calling* you to act in one particular scene, to go on an adventure.

Can you tell how that scene will turn out prior to engaging in it, or envision what subsequent scenes that chosen scene will open up for you?

Hell, no.

You simply have to leap and have faith.

And that's what frustrates the hell out of Coleridge. He hates not knowing what's going to happen next, because he wants your life to turn out the way *he* wants it to turn out; uneventful, painless and, especially, predictable, for you and for everyone around you. That's his job as your director.

The poet Shaemas O'Sheel wrote, "He whom a dream hath possessed knoweth no more of doubting."

But a dream can't possess you if you let Coleridge's aggressive, relentless chatter drown out the soft-spoken, yet inspirational voice of Keats. And trust me, Coleridge is tenacious. His self-concerned, controlling directives are very loud and extremely persuasive.

He's the voice of the world. And the world has a lot of things it wants you to be and to do.

Now, you don't *have* to listen to the quiet voice of Keats. No one really cares if you do. In fact, most people prefer that you don't. Except for the one person you've yet to meet. The most important person in your life, and the one who really cares if you listen to Keats or not.

Your future self. More specifically, your self at the end of your life.

Stephen Covey was right: to be highly effective begin with the end in mind. But to be effective *and* fulfilled, to live a life of purpose *and* passion, begin with *your* end in mind. And by your end, I mean your death. When you find Coleridge talking you out of something that's pulling you, something you really care about, ask yourself a simple question:

On my deathbed, will I look back on that decision favorably, because after all it may have turned out badly? I can assure you that you will not.

So instead, do as the poet Rumi advised and live life as if everything is rigged in your favor. Or you may wake up one day to discover that you never really lived.

Three

The privilege of a lifetime is being who you are.
— Joseph Campbell

You are a Kōan

A kōan is a statement that seems like a riddle.
One the reasoning mind can't solve.
So Zen Buddhists use them to *blow* people's minds.
And open up a crack to intuitive enlightenment.
A sudden, greater truth about life.
"What's the sound of one hand clapping?"
People think that's a kōan.
But I knew a guy in high school who solved it.
He raised one hand.
Relaxed his wrist and long fingers.
And then whipped the hell out of it.
Causing his flapping fingers to slap against his palm.
One hand clapping!
It was hilarious.

But that's not the actual kōan.
Instead, Hakuin Ekaku Zenji said:
"We all know that when we bring our two hands together sharply, they create a loud sound.
What is the sound of one hand?"
With all due respect to Zen orthodoxy, it really doesn't matter how it's phrased.
What matters is the spirit the kōan evokes.
And so the guy with the limber wrist?
He didn't know it, but he was enlightened.
He let his unique spirit emerge.
And everyone around him lightened up.
Here's something I bet *you* didn't know.
You are a kōan.
You sit and question who you are and what "it" is all about.
And your reasoning mind struggles.
Because it's an insoluble puzzle.
It's like pausing a movie before the end.
And trying to figure out what the protagonist is all about.
Who is this Dorothy Gale, really?
A lost, timid girl from Kansas?

What's she all about?
You can't tell.
So what really matters is her spirit.
What she evokes!
In herself and in others she encounters.
Because that's what illuminates everyone's journey.
Kierkegaard wrote, "Life is not a problem to be solved, but a reality to be experienced."
There you have it!
Life is a kōan.
And so are you.
So stop trying to solve it.
Crack open your hardened mind.
And let your unique spirit shine through.
Be who you are.
And let your essence ripple through eternity.

The Protagonist

The greatest screenplays on nearly everyone's list have one thing in common: they're stories about a particular individual, like Dorothy in *The Wizard of Oz*. And every major character and important scene in the movie revolves around that protagonist, like planets revolve around the sun.

This principle is extremely powerful, most likely because it connects deeply with our personal psychology.

We view life as though we are *its* central character, and everything and everyone in it revolves around us. Some believe this ego perspective—this sense of "me" or "I"—is the source of our worldly pain. If we'd just work to transcend this dream, this illusion of a separate self, we'd be set free from suffering.

The idea certainly feels right to me. I even intellectually subscribe to it, especially to the poet Rumi's beautiful sentiment:

"You are not a drop in the ocean. You are the entire ocean in a drop."

But I have one hell of a time maintaining that state of mind. It's like an optical illusion: you *know* that the spiral drawing is static, but you can't stop your eyes from *seeing* it move.

Let's face it: we're wired to believe our senses.

So perhaps we should stop fighting the dream and embrace it. Maybe it's not the *separate* self that haunts us at all but the *conditioned* self, the relentless voice of self-concern and speculation that keeps us ruminating in an invented story, instead of experiencing our impermanent dream to its absolute fullest.

Write Drunk

There's a quote flying around the Internet that's attributed to Ernest Hemingway: "Write drunk, edit sober." He never said it, but I like it anyway.

It implies that we need to call upon both Keats *and* Coleridge—feeling *and* thinking, inspiration *and* discipline—when creating our lives and our work. It's a balancing act, but one led by our values and our innermost feelings.

So ask yourself: What if I were to get drunk on the beauty and excitement of the world, instead of being under the intoxicating influence of my editing thoughts? What if I make Coleridge my servant, teach him to work *with* me, and only summons him when I really need him?

That's what *I am Keats*, as a philosophy, is all about: Magic, then logic. Heart, then head.

If we can pull it off and allow our inner voice to lead us—write drunk—our life will be an exciting and soulful one. One that serves both our self *and* the divine, the true source of our dream.

Because who's to say that the self, as that little drop, isn't the vehicle of the ocean. Perhaps the drop is the ocean's way of manifesting itself in the world.

Maybe, just maybe, you and I are the Universe's way of playing, creating scenes, and experiencing the amazing rush of being alive, of being a hero.

You are Its Hero

When you hear the word "hero," you probably imagine Superman or some other puffed up crusader. But in great stories, as in life, heroes are not a special type of person. They're ordinary people, like you and me and Dorothy. People who are swept up by circumstances, often reluctantly.

What makes them heroic is that they don't overthink things.

They don't judge, try to protect themselves, or use the situation to gain approval or success. Instead, they respond to circumstances by letting *Keats* lead, by doing what *feels* right in the moment. And that's what makes them so uncommon, and so precious.

I know what you're probably thinking:

"How do I know if what I'm feeling is 'right?' Maybe I should just ignore the voice and let the feeling pass."

I don't know about you, but I've spent a great part of my life ignoring my inner voice. Now I try not to by employing a simple heuristic. I ask myself a few quick questions and answer them with brutal honesty:

Is the voice I hear the voice of my curious, loving spirit? Am I responding to life, in the moment, by being true to that unique spirit and character? Will it provide me with a new experience? And, am I being as compassionate and caring, as possible, with the unique spirit and character of others?

They are Their Heroes

I find that last question to be the most challenging, because one of the most difficult things to appreciate, as the central character of your own life, is that others are the central characters of theirs.

As William James remarked: “mankind's common instinct for reality . . . has always held the world to be essentially a theatre for heroism.”

And from others' perspective, *you* are one of the supporting characters in *their* heroic journeys.

You revolve around them.

So how can you be the conscious hero of your own life, while being a supporting character in other people's lives? How can you lift people up and give them faith in their own potential, inspire them to be truly alive, and let them experience their unique, unfolding lives while, at the same time, allowing your inner spirit to evolve and direct you?

It's a daunting challenge because we want others to be what we want them to be, primarily to support us in our particular scene. So how do we relieve that tension?

It's so simple and yet so damn hard: Shut down Coleridge. Give up the need to be right and to control the scene.

Coleridge is trying to keep you focused on *your* character and on *your* wants and needs, including the ones he imagines can be satisfied by others.

But people aren't here to be your supporting characters, so don't project your director onto them. Give them control. Let go of narrative thinking and your egotistical role and realize that your scene is yours, and their scenes are theirs.

Suspension of Disbelief

And here's another paradox:

If you don't shut down Coleridge, he will write and direct your life to suit everyone *but* you.

He'll keep you alienated, depressed and pressured, out of touch with your unique inner spirit, relentlessly telling you who you are, how to think, and what to say and do in order to maintain control, conform and be accepted. He'll skillfully work to keep you busy and distracted, totally immersed "in character," in order to maintain a story that keeps you, and everyone else, willingly suspended in disbelief.

That strange phrase, "willing suspension of disbelief," was coined by Samuel Taylor Coleridge to describe the relationship between an audience and a work of fiction.

The audience "knows" what they're reading or watching is "only a story," yet they suspend that knowledge and act as if they are experiencing something real. And so people cry at the end of *Toy Story 3*, or recoil at the mechanical shark in the classic thriller *Jaws*.

Believe it or not, that same thing is happening to you with your life.

You "know," in your gut, that it's invented, that it's *really* a story and that you don't have to be moved by your director, the other actors, or the audience. But you've become so wrapped up in it that you've completely forgotten that it's all make-believe, and that you can make something completely different whenever you choose.

Screenplays have to make sense to keep audiences engaged and "suspended." And so stories follow a particular model, a script that draws people in deeper and deeper.

In fact, the movie industry is overflowing with frameworks and consultants to help you do just that. And anything that you write that draws the audience out, that lets them glimpse reality, is painstakingly avoided.

Stories are Coherent

But life *isn't* a screenplay and it *doesn't* have to make sense. You don't have to be defined and confined by your his*tory*, your present situation, or by social roles. You're not a character in a serious script that must remain consistent, coherent and predictable.

Yes your mind *wants* your life to make sense, to feel as though it's an evolving story. But that's simply your director, Coleridge, working you to follow your script, so that you internalize society's values and support the roles of the other actors.

He wants your story to flow.

And what ties a story together and makes it flow? Two persistent and potent illusions: the past —the backstory—which defines the characters' emotions and behaviors, and the future—the narrative arc and ending—which provides continuity and the ultimate emotional payoff. In fact, the ending is typically the whole point of a story:

"There's no place like home."

Guess what?

The end of your life is *not* the point of your life, and your backstory does *not* dictate your future. But your life director, Coleridge, makes you *believe* that it does. He works really hard to eliminate anything, any behavior or scene, that may confuse you, your audience, or the other actors and *knock* everyone out of their suspension of disbelief.

It's the most compelling illusion in the world, and the most dangerous. Because you're crafting your life under the same limiting construct as a screenplay and you don't even know it.

Phil Doesn't Exist

How powerful is that illusion?

During the writing of the screenplay, Shannon suggested that one of our lead characters, Phil, take a particular course of action to make the story even more compelling and entertaining. But I had an immediate and viscerally negative reaction to her idea:

"What the hell are you talking about?! Phil would never do that!"

Pause and really think about that exchange for a moment: "Phil" doesn't even exist! We made him up, and so we could have decided to make him do anything we wanted him to do.

But we *couldn't* because, based on how we defined Phil's character, it felt totally wrong. We knew in our guts that the narrative wouldn't retain its verisimilitude, and stay congruent and acceptable to the audience.

And so we nixed the idea.

That same illusory feeling will edit *your* life and nix *your* ideas, if you let it. It will repress your inner spirit and direct you to stay "in character," for both your supporting characters and for your audience. You will become hypnotized, your inner voice tranquilized, causing you to live in a consistent manner, true to your contrived past and to your comforting projection of the future.

In due time, clinging to that static story and to your rigid goals will define you, making you a caricature of yourself, a cliché. Sadly, you'll find yourself compulsively going through the motions and totally annihilating your authentic character.

Authentic Character

Authentic character sounds like an oxymoron, like act naturally. The word "character" is derived from engraved markings in printing and was later used, metaphorically, to mean the qualities that define a person.

If those qualities emanate from your script, from your externally influenced identity, from Coleridge, you'll be restrained by memories of your past and self-referential ideas of the future.

But if it springs from your intuitive self, from Keats, from the awareness that the past and future are powerfully hypnotic stories, you'll be set free to live authentically.

The word "authentic" comes from "original, possessing authority." To be authentic means to be your "self" (aut), to stop denying your uniqueness, fire Coleridge, and be the author and director of your own life.

Yes, you should be aware of the scene you're in, and to the fact that others believe themselves to be heroes in their illusional and delusional stories. But let Keats direct you, and then you can direct Coleridge to work *with* Keats, to help achieve an acceptable scene.

It's a balance; authentic *and* effective.

And the paradox, as a conditioned and scripted human being, is that your self only becomes authentic when it is consciously constructed. You're not being authentic unless you're *aware* that you're being authentic, that Keats is leading you in a considered, yet unselfconscious way.

Four

All of us have wonders hidden in our breasts, only needing circumstances to evoke them.

— Charles Dickens

Serendipity as Strategy

We crave certainty.

I know that I do.

We want to believe that everything will turn out okay.

That everyone will be... fine.

(I almost wrote "happy.")

And that's why we resist change.

Not because we dislike change.

You can't dislike something you can't imagine.

Rather, we dislike the scary unknown.

Despite pithy quotes like Eleanor Roosevelt's.

"Do one thing every day that scares you."

We seldom do anything that truly scares us.

Instead, we submit and simply work longer and harder at what we already know.

At what "works."
And hope like hell that everything will be alright.
Human beings have built in, unconscious
aversions towards risk.
So we choose the safest option.
And what appears safest is what's immediate and
visceral.
What's in our grasp and right in front of our eyes.
Why?
Because we don't want to lose what we already
have.
Our position, status, money, lifestyle.
So we hold on tight.
Which means that most of us are tethered.
To what we're grasping.
To our beliefs, our stories.
To routine and dependence.
To a life of foolish consistency.
And so we'll never fly high and free.
But there is an option.
Aimless wandering.
I'm being quite sincere.
Cut the damn cord, at least temporarily.

Place yourself in a strange environment.
Pick up a random book and read it.
Start a relationship with someone who fascinates you.
Volunteer at a non-profit.
Yes, we all want to live authentic lives.
But authenticity isn't about what you choose to do.
It's about how you choose to do it.
So get out there and do something, anything, new.
Stop trying to figure it all out.
Stop trying to protect yourself from an unknowable future.
Instead be a connected and passionate part of the here and now.
Let serendipity be your new strategy.
And watch it unfold your unique destiny.

Destiny or Fate

Carl Jung claimed, "Until you make the unconscious conscious, it will direct your life and you will call it fate."

That unconscious director is Coleridge, and fate is what happens when you follow the script and passively succumb to what he tosses at you. But if you listen to your essence, to the voice of Keats, it will alter your fate and create your unique destiny.

The ancient Greek philosopher Heraclitus wrote, "Ethos anthropos daimon."

Most translations suggest it means, "Character is fate." Others say it means, "Character is destiny." It's another paradox, because it's both: "Character is fate" if that character is the artificially constructed, scripted character of society. But "character is destiny" if it's your authentic character, your inner spirit.

Consider the great Socrates who chose to drink the hemlock, rather than flee, in order to be faithful to his "daimon," his unique inner voice. His decision to examine his life, to make the unconscious conscious, is what *destined* him to greatness, inspiring countless thinkers and exerting a profound influence on modern philosophy.

Everyone's fate is known; we all die. There's no way of saving ourselves.

It's our destiny that's unknown, because no one can predict the outcome of his or her actions. Destiny emerges and then flows through the world like blood through a body.

Do you know where your blood flow begins and ends? Have you any idea what it nourishes and how? Of course not, because it's natural and dynamic.

And so are you.

So why can't you simply flow with your essence and nourish the world with your uniqueness? That's the challenge with serendipity. You have no idea how your choices will flourish and affect your future, or the lives of others, but they most surely will. You also don't know which random circumstances will evoke Keats, in you and in others, and expose you to those serendipitous encounters.

It's interesting: We trust our body—the most incredible and complex structure on earth—to get us through life. But we just can't seem to relax and trust our self.

Two Persistent Questions

Whenever I share my serendipitous *I am Keats* journey, two requests invariably confront me:

"Tell me about the strange occurrences," and "Tell me how you did it."

People want to hear an engaging story and they want to imagine a predictable path. This appears to be how we're wired. We want to believe we can orchestrate "success" through knowledge and hard work, and that luck and serendipity have little or nothing to do with it.

Tellingly, I was asked by many in the movie industry if I followed *their* simple path; Joseph

Campbell's *Hero's Journey* monomyth. I was certainly aware of it but I didn't consciously employ it, because I wasn't really writing the story.

It was writing me.

I am Keats was birthed by an internal impulse and nurtured by serendipity. There was nothing straightforward about it, and that's what confuses people and makes them suspicious.

It's quite revealing as well that, while researching *The Hero's Journey,* I found Joseph Campbell rarely, if ever, mouthed or wrote the words luck or serendipity. In fact, in a search of his seminal work of comparative mythology, *The Hero with a Thousand Faces,* the word "luck" appears a mere half-dozen times and "serendipity" is nowhere to be found.

It appears that the stories human beings invent and tell, especially about heroic journeys, are devoid of the actual randomness of life. It's probably because stories are nothing more than manufactured beliefs and, like movies, they need to be clear and coherent. They're designed to grab us and hypnotically string us along, while artfully concealing their inherent messiness.

That's our truth. And, although truth is transitory, that particular one appears to be immutable.

Don't Just Sit There

And here's another truth:

"Success" is simply another story that we're telling ourselves, and we're hypnotized into believing that there's a clear, unambiguous path to achieving it.

First, there's nothing straightforward about this advanced illusion called life. It's a challenging series of dilemmas and tensions, and as Marcus Aurelius pointed out, "Everything we hear is an opinion, not a fact. Everything we see is a perspective, not the truth."

And, to confuse you more, there is no path because there's nowhere to go.

Imagine being plopped down in the middle of a vast and strange amusement park overflowing with amazing sights and sounds, and alive with fantastic people and experiences. If you stop someone and ask which of the myriad paths in the park you should take, they'll invariably respond, "Well, what do you like? What interests you?"

And now you're faced with a dilemma. You don't *know* what you like, because you haven't *experienced* it yet. And all of the information in the world won't help, because concepts are vague without experience.

Plus, it's all opinion and perspective anyway.

So, if you want to experience life, you have to be Keats, pick a path, and explore the park "in uncertainties, mysteries, doubts." And that's scary. So much so that most people will simply plop down in one place and remain there, perplexed.

I've been saying for years that people don't fear change. What we fear is the unknown, or surrendering the known, and listening to Keats is what brings us that uncertainty. We become fearful and anxious, especially about falling behind and losing our wealth and status. The mere thought threatens our manufactured identity, as well as the secure and comfortable cell of routine that protects our self-esteem and gives us a satisfying, albeit delusional, sense of control over life.

And it's that refuge of routine that digs us deeper into our ruts and drains the living Keats out of us.

Like caged animals, it dulls our senses to the reality of the changing world, stunts our growth, and makes us feel lethargic and impotent.

So why don't we do something about it and change our fate? Because Coleridge keeps Keats hypnotized, asleep at the wheel.

Newton's law of inertia states that a body at rest will remain at rest unless an outside force acts on it (like a truck blasting its horn). And that brings us to one of the most interesting and critical elements of a screenplay, and of life.

The Inciting Incident

The inciting incident is an event at the beginning of a movie that jolts the central character out of her everyday routine and compels her to take some type of action. It's an external force beyond her will or control (fate) that stimulates an internal force (intention) and drives her story and character development forward (destiny).

A tornado whisks Dorothy to a foreign land, which compels her to get back home and sets her on an exciting journey of discovery.

There's a lot of debate over when the inciting incident should occur in a movie with most agreeing that the earlier it occurs, the better. But no one questions its significance, because there is no actual story until it happens. The inciting incident is what emotionally grabs the audience and drags them in.

Great stories also employ conflict and loss, obstacles and opportunities, passion and tension, and mysteries and acts of faith; events most human beings are desperate to avoid.

On his blog, the American screenwriter John August makes clear, "If characters were allowed to control their scenes, most characters would choose to avoid conflict, and movies would be crushingly boring."

And that's because the characters would be getting their direction from Coleridge, and he couldn't care less if their lives are crushingly boring. Sure, Coleridge knows that inciting incidents, obstacles and conflict are what make life exciting and instructive, but that causes him problems as your director. He's thoroughly resolved to keep the script—the status quo—intact and predictable, and for that reason he will not tolerate any ad-libbing.

Incite Yourself

"Ad-lib" is short for "ad-libitum," which is Latin for "at one's pleasure." Coleridge discourages you from pursuing anything new, anything "at your pleasure," for fear that it might incite you and disrupt the flow of the story. So stop waiting for your practical mind to *logically incite* you (it's oxymoronic). Your reasoning mind will never calmly direct you to step out of your role and to be daring and impractical.

One of the most famous lines in the movie *Lawrence of Arabia* declares, "Truly for some men nothing is written unless they write it." In today's modern world that reality is true of *most* people. Their Keats' minds have been seduced by the script, by dependency and comfort, and it typically takes something traumatic to wake them up. And then, as in all great stories, they'll do what truly moves them.

If you look closely you'll find that most movies eventually show the hero as we wish *we* could be. But here's the thing:

We don't have to wish for it.

We can experience it, whenever we finally realize that every setback and disaster we survived was something we needed to improve our character. Screenwriters understand this reality—that Coleridge has people under his spell —and that's why they incite their characters and *push* them through crisis and disaster towards their destinies.

So why can't we become our own directors and incite ourselves? Why should we wait to be pushed by tragedy or misfortune? Why can't we consciously break the trance of comfort and routine by listening to Keats and ad-libbing our way towards our destinies?

I'll tell you why:

As soon as we get a feeling for something new, we freeze up. Coleridge kicks in and anxiously tries to script the future to ensure a positive outcome. This relentless need to know what will happen next is paralyzing, and it's the source of most of our suffering. It enslaves us in a mental cage of hard-headed materialism and snuffs out serendipity.

But it's a delusional cage, because it's impossible to script the unknown. The future is dynamic; it's perpetually moving and changing. We have to step into it to see where it takes us.

And that's what makes life exciting!

A Dancing Flower

One of our most stifling, yet imperceptible mental cages is our mechanistic, Newtonian model of reality; Coleridge's linear cause-and-effect thinking. We feel that we are *causing* everything in our life to happen.

Just like a screenplay, we feel a continuous and causal connection between our backstory, our present situation and actions, and our ultimate future. It's a dangerous, anxiety-producing illusion, and we invent it as a natural extension of our self-story.

Think of yourself as a dancing flower (I know, just go with me on this one.) You could either say that you—the flower—*cause* butterflies to move towards you. Or you could say that butterflies *value* movement towards you.

Scientifically speaking, both statements are exactly the same. But metaphorically speaking, they are very different. To believe that you cause things to move towards you implies certainty and control. To believe that things value movement towards you implies preference and chance.

If you adopt cause-and-effect thinking, you'll adhere to the script. You'll plant yourself in one place and follow formulaic thinking and behavior, even in the face of dissatisfaction and a changing environment.

Even worse, you'll close up. You'll constantly question and judge yourself, wondering if you're good enough, smart enough, have tried hard enough, and every other Coleridge-induced limiting thought. Eventually, you'll end up feeling weak and desperate and, despite your intentions, you'll come across that way to others as well. Yet another paradox:

The harder you try to make things happen, the more elusive they become.

But once you realize that the world is chaotic and dynamic, that no one is "in control" and that it's simply the Universe (or the divine, God, or whatever you choose to call the invisible force behind the mystery of existence) doing *its* dance of desire, you'll stop chasing your future. You'll relax, open up your beautiful flower, jump in and join the dance.

That's how you spark serendipity.

Live from the inside out and give full expression to the gift that has come to you—your unique essence and ideas. And then dance with that passionate spirit in as many diverse fields as possible. Unfold your delicate petals, your center of being, and the butterflies may come.

Do You Have the Nerve?

But what if nothing happens? What if the butterflies don't show up? What if no one dances with me?

And around and around we go: "I feel like…" "But what if…?"

Pick one!

Live your life as an exclamation mark, true to your deepest internal callings, or live it as a question mark. It's your choice, and one of the few that you actually have any control over. And I can assure you that twenty years from now, it will be the only decision you'll wish you could do over. So, do you have the nerve to be you?

It's another paradox and one of life's most difficult: Live as a exclamation mark, as Keats, and you'll be vulnerable. The questioning world of Coleridge will probably reject you.

But, that tension is what makes you feel most alive.

Why?

Because it comes with Keats' transcendent pleasure, his childlike learning and creation. And that sets you free and gives you a life that stretches your inherent capabilities and stirs your passions. Plus, do you really think that your odds for success and happiness improve by toeing the line and hoping for things to change?

Go grab a rubber band. I'll wait.

Now loop it around both of your thumbs and stretch it out as far as it will go, right in front of your face. Keep stretching it until it feels like it's going to snap.

Hold it there.

Can you feel that tension? That's the tension you'll experience, in your mind, between Keats—faith in your inner voice—and Coleridge—belief in the stories you're telling yourself.

F. Scott Fitzgerald wrote, "The test of a first-rate intelligence is the ability to hold two opposed ideas in mind at the same time and still retain the ability to function."

That's the paradoxical underpinning of negative capability.

We can either be Keats and venture out into uncertainty, create amazing scenes, and tolerate the ambiguity and confusion. Or we can live a more tedious, restrained existence, and get our feelings from a simulated world of safe, manufactured stories.

I am not suggesting that there is a right way or wrong way to live. One hundred and eight billion people have lived on the planet and each chose a different way to live.

Your job is to discover *your* way, your truest self, and then make choices that release that essence, share your unique message, and create an exciting and meaningful life.

Howard Thurman had it right: "Don't ask what the world needs. Ask what makes you come alive and go do it."

The reality is that most people *will* relentlessly ask the world what it needs, stay in their roles and follow their scripts. And that's okay. But there are others, a select few, who should soar and create amazing lives and amazing scenes. And for no other reason than because it's inside of them and it needs to come out, to benefit themselves, the world, and those other passionate souls like them.

Frankly, I can't think of a better reason. And if you've read this far, you're probably one of those select few.

Five

The future is always beginning now.

— Mark Strand

Life is Improv

"Put your hand on a hot stove for a minute, and it seems like an hour.

Sit with a pretty girl for an hour, and it seems like a minute."

According to Einstein, "THAT'S relativity."

Time is simply a way of *relating* various events.

The future doesn't exist.

It isn't an integral part of a present that unfolds.

And the past isn't something that's in the books.

It isn't settled.

It's invented as we go.

What the past means depends on what we're experiencing now.

Miles Davis put it this way:

"When you hit a wrong note, it's the next note that makes it good or bad."

It's like a sentence.
The meaning of the words depend on the words that follow.
Gaze into your significant other's eyes and say, "Honey, I love…"
You can either end that sentence with "you" or, say, "donuts."
And surely your choice will change the meaning of the word "love."
To say nothing of the reaction and subsequent unfolding.
But the unfolding isn't predetermined.
There is no script.
It will be created by you, in that moment.
The past doesn't create the present.
Your present creates the meaning of your past.
George Bernard Shaw wrote, "We are made wise not by the recollection of our past, but by the responsibility for our future."
Rather, we are made wise by the recognition that there is no past, nor future.
There is only the stream of experience we call "[illegible]w."

Life is improv and now is it.
Each moment is all there is.
And how we master those moments is our real responsibility.

Life's not Scripted

If life was thought out and scripted would a tall man be paid $90,000 an hour to toss a ball through a hoop, while another earns less than $9 an hour risking his life in a foreign land to defend that man's freedom?

Would a writer get $100,000 to give a half hour talk about his latest book, while it takes a typical teacher two long years to make that same amount? Would a DJ make $300,000 for a single night's work in a dance club, while during those same six hours a neonatal nurse makes $200?

Not unless life is an absurd comedy, which it may be. I'm not really sure. But I am sure of this: In a free society, there's no one in control of how, and to what, human beings assign value.

Mark Twain wrote, "When we remember that we are all mad, the mysteries disappear and life stands explained."

That madness is Coleridge, our mental conditioning, and it manifests itself in the stories we compose—stories that have been sown into the ground of our consciousness and which drive our decisions and shape our world.

And that same madness creates our personal identity, our safe cage of character.

Look back over your life and it will appear as orderly, consistent, and sentimental as a composed narrative. We describe periods of our lives as if they were "chapters"—like our sandlot years and college days. That's because our minds are wired to create meaning and structure out of a fragmented and complicated tangle of connections, to string random twists and turns into causally-linked sets of events.

Emerson once remarked that there is properly no history, only biography. The stories we create about the past aren't the Truth (with a capital T). They're a personal fiction, the mind's meaning-making apparatus at work.

But, like most everything the mind creates, it affects us.

We end up living in those stories, and according to them. And our desire for Coleridge to direct us in those fantasies is a profound psychological need to feel special and in control. And so eventually our lives become bland and routine, or else an anxiety-filled existence of measurement and comparison. All because of an illusional story.

We Just Don't Know

Have you ever created a story about some aspect of your life and later discovered that someone lied to you, making it all a distressing illusion?

I have.

When we experience this sudden powerlessness, it can feel devastating. And that's because we've temporarily lost control of our narrative, of our expectations and overwhelming desire for continuity. We don't know where we're heading, or who or what to believe.

On the other hand, if we *believe* we know what's happening around us, especially the near term future and general direction, we feel safe and in control. That's why we resist change and want our agendas and ideologies to prevail. It gives us the comforting feeling of knowing how things will turn out, assuring us that we have the knowledge and experience to survive and, hopefully, to thrive.

Of course, it's all a comforting illusion. "Actual life is full of false clues and signposts that lead nowhere," E.M. Forster once wrote.

We believe we know what others are thinking and what will eventually happen, but we don't. Research has found that even parents can't tell if their kids are lying more than fifty percent of the time. We read minds and time travel in order to feel good about our *imagined* scripts and allay our anxieties.

Five hundred years ago, Michel de Montaigne said, "My life has been filled with terrible misfortune; most of which never happened."

Misfortune or fortune, what happens in life has little to do with the stories we endlessly spin. And believe it or not, what happens also has little to do with our conscious decisions. We're unaware of our swarm of cognitive biases, our mental faults and limitations, and even if we were conscious of them we simply don't have the time or energy to consider them. And so most of the time, we're being pushed and pulled by our environment and our instincts.

But we imagine otherwise.

We create a meaning-infused narrative to rationalize that we are autonomous, significant individuals—free to be ourselves and entitled to have our imagined futures of fame and fortune realized.

Hope But Don't Expect

When you meet with someone do you know precisely what you are going to say or how it will turn out? When you get ready to play a game do you know exactly what you are going to do or what the result will be? When you have a new idea do you know, without a doubt, what will happen if you pursue it?

Of course not.

You may have a vision and even a plan, but you don't actually "know" what will happen. No one does. Expectations are simply more soothing stories that Coleridge tells us about our future to keep us calm and in our place. They're mental illusions, but ones that can have devastating effects on your life.

Do you remember the Greek myth about Pandora (not the streaming music service, the first woman created by the Gods)? She was given a box (actually a jar) and was instructed to never open it. Fat chance.

Anyway, out flew all the evils of humanity; hate, pain, disease, Internet popup ads. When Pandora was aware of what she had done, she quickly closed the jar, and trapped one item inside. Do you know what it was?

Elpis (hope)!

But why hope? Is hope evil, like the other contents? Nietzsche thought so. He called hope the worst of all evils, "because it prolongs the torments of man." I appreciate where Friedrich was coming from; I'm also predisposed to scoff at hope and to face up to the realities of life. But I see it a bit differently.

Hope is a double-edged sword.

It can be evil, especially when it keeps us on a misguided path; one that causes us to live a disengaged or inauthentic life, and which inevitably gives rise to the other evils in that jar (burdensome toil, regret, and despair). But hope truly is a paradox, because hope also helps us remain optimistic and push forward in the face of adversity and setbacks.

David Mamet wrote, "We all hope. It's what keeps us alive." And he's right. But being alive and living an authentic, inspired life are quite different. Hope can blind us to a suppressed existence and keep us blissfully numb. To be fully alive, we must know when to abandon hope, when to smash the jar of conjecture on the hard ground of reality, embrace our individuality, change course, and allow unexpected possibilities to create life anew.

Hope isn't evil; it's another tension.

We need hope to move us to pursue our desires, create something new, and change the world. Rather, it's the expectation that it will turn out the way we want it to that torments us. So deal with the reality of life and treat it like you do any other game; play it with passion and with the sincere hope that you will win, that you will get the results and the world you want.

But never *expect* that you will.

Life Happens in Each Moment

Life is enormously complex and the environment and people we interact with are extremely complicated. And so are we. Therefore, we have no real choice *but* to hope and to improvise. But you'd never know that based on the stories we tell ourselves, stories which appear to mimic the ones we create and share with each other.

Consider a movie, which is a tense and taut cause-and-effect construction. What happens in one scene determines what happens in later scenes, and everything that happens has a definitive purpose. Screenwriters obsess over every image, word and action so that it moves the story forward, from the unexpected opening scene until the cathartic ending, in an engaging and cohesive way. Every dot is connected, nothing is random. In fact, the ending of the movie is what typically informs the very beginning.

Life isn't like that at all. It isn't a purposeful construction with a central thesis. Stuff just happens.

And that's why it's so challenging to create a film biography about a real person. The filmmaker digs into the character's life and discovers a bunch of random events rather than a cohesive drama. And so he must decide what period of the person's life to highlight, which scenes to include and exclude, and in what order to present those scenes for dramatic effect. When the biography eventually makes it to the big screen, the entire story of that person's life ends up looking deliberate and heroic.

It's a lie, unless, as George Costanza said, you believe it.

It's funny, if you ask screenwriters for advice on how to write a great screenplay, they'll get all Coleridge with you and give you *their* script—the ten steps to success, Campbell's *Hero's Journey*, and other logical frameworks and templates.

But ask someone how he or she wrote such a successful screenplay and suddenly it becomes a Keatsian affair with serendipitous encounters, ideas from the Muse, and a whole lot of intuition and improvisational writing.

Don't let the stories people tell fool you. Success is really more a matter of courage than knowledge. All the information in the world is no substitute for the guts to follow Keats.

Unscripted and Unselfconscious

In improvisational theatre the characters, dialogue and action are created collaboratively, in real time.

In one scene you may be a lost child, and in the next a criminal on the run.

Most actors hate improv, because they fear the lack of control and the effort required to be fully present and attentive.

Improv takes guts.

Improv is creation on the fly, during the actual performance. There's no script or director and so you have to perform without a net, stripped of the comfort of your "character."

Those skilled at improv relish the spontaneity, the chance conversations, experiences, and interactions. It's a relief since, realizing that it has no idea where the scene is going, their frenetic Coleridge minds give up and surrender to Keats. And then their Keats and Coleridge minds work together, in harmony, to create scene enhancing dialogue and action. The result being a suspension of thought, a contemplative awareness, and an exemplar of negative capability.

Why?

Because negative capability is an attentive state of mind. It's marked by a receptive openness, an unscripted and unselfconscious acceptance of "what is." Whatever happens, happens. You don't analyze it, judge it, or interfere with it. You accept the full-scale experience for what it is, in the moment.

And acceptance doesn't mean resignation to what's happening. It means being situationally aware, both internally and externally, knowing what's going on, what you are doing, and moving in the direction that Keats tells you to move, with alert interest and with resolve. You deal with the situation, and then build off of it.

Authentic and effective.

Dynamic or Static

Keats also argued that one who possesses negative capability "has no Identity—he is continually informing and filling some other Body." These "Men of Genius" are chameleons, able to disregard their own self-interest and direct their attention to the object or the other, and thus open themselves up to a much vaster inner world than the ones of their scripted characters.

Negative capability promotes empathy and expands one's consciousness.

So yes, life is improv. It's dynamic. You toss ideas into the world and you learn from, and play off of, the reaction. Story is static. You follow the script and stay steadfastly in character.

If you're practicing improv, you're engaged in life, swimming in a sea of wonder and experiencing each moment non-judgmentally, with empathy, fully awake to the possibilities as they unfold. You deal with each situation with the reaction that's needed to cause something heartfelt to happen.

And then, regardless of the outcome, you let that moment go knowing that the future will take care of itself.

If you're stuck in your story, you're wrapped up in a hyper-anxious dreamworld of self-concern and control. You react to circumstances based on your story, on the way you want things to be or the way that they used to be for you. And you carry each moment with you, either as a validation of, or an affront to, your personal fiction and your significance as the script's central character.

Players or Characters

The most important difference between staged improv and life is the state of mind and intention of the participants.

Improv players are working together to lift each other *out* of traditional roles and put themselves in touch with the situation, their authentic selves, and each other. Players never reject what's presented. Instead they say yes, and contribute something to the scene. Everyone's sincere intent is total involvement with the other, without judgment, to create an intuitive, holistic experience.

And this full embrace of what's happening in the moment creates a sense of cooperation, affirmation, and fun.

Sadly, life doesn't often work that way. And that's because most people aren't awake and aware. They're hypnotized by their stories and anxiously protective of their roles. They're not conscious, sincere players; they're entranced, serious characters whose parts are playing them. And they want *you* to go to sleep, join in on the drama, and support their seriously delusional stories.

Don't do it.

An Absurd Script

I recently discovered a used book by Emily Holt, copyright 1901. The title, and especially the ridiculous subtitle, blew my mind:

Encyclopaedia of Etiquette: What to Do. What to Say. What to Write. What to Wear. A Book of Manners for Everyday Use.

It's an absurd handbook on how to be an acceptable character. But here's something more absurd:

If you look closely, you'll discover that same absurdity everywhere you look.

We "learn" from each other precisely what to do, what to say, what to wear, what to eat, what to own, where to work, where to live, how to look, how to feel, who to love, in essence, how to think and what to believe. And we call that made up script "culture."

It doesn't feel made up; it feels real, as though we're significant characters in serious roles. And its allures are pervasive and seductive, because we're always being coached or corrected by the world.

Sadly, most of us internalize that script—the various socio-cultural expectations and labels—solidifying the notion that we are characters in a very important story. And we act out those roles in strangely, hypnotic ways. This classic line from the movie *Fight Club* contains much more truth than fiction:

"We buy things we don't need, to impress people we don't like."

Connected and Hooked

It's undeniable, we are social creatures.

Our very survival depended upon getting people's attention and approval, on being coached and corrected. We cried for food and warmth, and we smiled and performed for affection and reward. And we quickly learned the way things are done, all of the social norms and standards of behavior that would keep us safe, satisfy our needs and achieve our goals. And now we're hooked.

But, we've taken it way too far.

As a wise Rabbi once said, "If I am I because you are you. And you are you because I am I. Then I am not I and you are not you." Indeed, everything and everyone is connected. We are not separate. We define each other.

I may be a writer but without you, a reader, I don't really exist. So it's important for me to use intellect and compassion to understand how you read and to conform when it's functional, like having this book written in your native language or in a desirable font.

But those Coleridge calculations are secondary to my Keatsian spirit, to my essence, to my creations and my unique needs. Yes, I follow the script of culture when necessary, but I also know that it's all an invention. And so I'm free to reject societal assumptions concerning what I need or what I'm supposed to be doing, and intelligently deal with the possible consequences.

Clearly, working together is an unavoidable part of modern life. Unfortunately most of us take the silly script for granted, compulsively conforming and never questioning the underlying assumptions. We end up performing our way through life.

And most people love that we willingly adopt and passively remain in our limiting roles; the ones we've created for ourselves (with their help).

The Conclusion of Thinking

Do you have any idea what all of those cultural norms—the scripted stories, characters, roles and rules—do to you once you've passively adopted and internalized them?

They enclose you in a thick, invisible box of beliefs.

During an interview about my last book, someone asked me to define belief and to do so "succinctly." So I answered, "Belief is simply the story in your head." My casual response gave him pause.

"What story is that?" he asked.

I replied, matter-of-factly, "What ever story you're telling yourself, to rationalize your feelings and behavior."

He stared at me, a bemused look on his face. So I did what I do. I asked him some pointed questions. Ones designed to wake him up and illuminate the answer.

"Do you like steak?" I began.

"I do," he replied.

"And do you ever think about the cow?"

Long pause. "Do you see?" I continued. "The cow is not part of your 'steak story.' In your story, a steak exists as a separate thing. In fact, in your story steaks have special names. Names which convey meaning and value to you, like tenderloin, porterhouse and ribeye. But I'll bet you have no idea if the cow had a name."

He had had enough. He got my point.

Here's the thing about our beliefs. We don't want them pointed out to us. We don't want to have our soothing stories interrupted. We don't want to be woken up from our script, from our reassuring routines. Otherwise, we'll have to think. And then, heaven forbid, we may have to change.

Shannon is fond of saying, "Belief is the conclusion of thinking." And conclusions are the ultimate comfort.

Make no mistake: culture's script limits your thoughts and your potential. It shelters you from life, distorting your perceptions, eliminating choice and free will, and preventing you from discovering your truest self and living with a fullness of being. And that's what causes perpetual discontent, a lack of creativity, and the slow suffocation of your spirit.

So yes, Bob Dylan was right, "Everybody's got to serve somebody." Our common myths are what have allowed us to thrive as a species. But that doesn't have to alienate you from your authentic self. Just be very conscious of who that somebody is, and make absolutely sure that he or she or them, in turn, is serving you and your unique spirit.

Choose Your Scene

Short of living alone in a hut like Thoreau, it's virtually impossible to block out the deluge of socio-cultural messages. Despite your awareness, you simply can not resist the influence of your environment. Trust me, I've tried. Therefore, choosing that environment, your various scenes, is one of the most important decisions you can make. Because your inner spirit wants to lose itself in something larger than itself, an idea it really cares about, which can be shared with others.

So what is a scene?

Right now, there's a digital economy scene going on in places like Mountain View, Menlo Park, San Francisco, and Beijing.

The movie making scene is presently happening in cities like L.A., Austin, Chicago, and New York.

In the 1860s, the first modern art scene emerged in Paris. We now refer to those innovative malcontents, people like Paul Cézanne, Camille Pissarro, and Édouard Manet, as impressionists.

The beat scene, which heavily influenced American culture and brought us the literary works of people like Allen Ginsberg, William S. Burroughs, and Jack Kerouac, blossomed in Greenwich Village in the 1950s.

There are also various sports scenes (Vegas for boxing), music scenes (Memphis blues), and food scenes (Napa for wine). A scene is a location where people of similar desires and worldviews gather. It's a richly interdependent community of talents and opportunities. And due to the power and ubiquity of the Internet, many scenes are now taking place online. We have an amazing scene blossoming at www.iamkeats.com.

But there are also work scenes, drug scenes, bar scenes, and gang scenes. The key to choosing a scene, to deciding whether or not to enter one, stay in one, or move on from one, is to ask yourself:

Are these people and experiences inspiring my best self, my Keats? Are they sincere players, or a bunch of serious characters? Is there a heartfelt exchange of ideas and support of each other's uniqueness and passions?

If so, stay and grow. But if not, if you've been fooled too many times, move on.

Do you know that expression: Fool me once, shame on you; fool me twice, shame on me?

If you ever find that you've been fooled *three* times, get the hell off of that stage and out of that scene. Life is too short to suffer self-induced frustration. Get away from those characters, and find some players who will shine a light on your unique spirit, enliven your passions, and help release your amazing potential.

Tom Petty was spot on: "You belong somewhere you'll feel free."

Six

We cannot be more sensitive to pleasure without being more sensitive to pain.

— Alan Watts

The Process is the Goal

I watched a beautiful little film called *Still Mine*.
It's based on a true story about 89-year-old New Brunswicker Craig Morrison.
Morrison sets out on a journey to build a more suitable house for his ailing wife.
Using the same methods his shipbuilder father taught him.
But on the way, he runs into problem after problem after problem.
After watching the film, and wiping away a tear, I thought a lot about struggle and accomplishment.
I remember, as a boy, accompanying boxers to an inner city gym.
I'd watch them pridefully endure horrible conditions and physical torture.

Finally realizing that their hardship was an integral, and desirable, part of their identity.

Later in life, I saw comedians bomb.

Artists destroy hours of painstaking work.

Writers, including yours truly, paralyzed in a fog of doubt.

But the best endured.

Because they loved the process.

They were one with the work.

They had something they had to "get across" to the world.

Thomas Mann wrote, "A writer is someone for whom writing is more difficult than it is for other people."

That's true of everyone on an inspired journey.

Basketball was more difficult for Michael Jordan.

Politics was more difficult for Abraham Lincoln.

Civil rights advocacy was more difficult for Dr. King.

Teaching the truth of our humanity was more difficult for Jesus.

The greatest don't see an endpoint.

They're driven by the realities of the here and now.

By the process, not the proceeds.

For them, the struggle is an integral part of their journeys.

In fact, and they probably don't even know it, the process is their goal.

For the journey and the outcome are one and the same.

No Pain No Change

I've been privy to the lifestyles and routines of scores of athletes—weight lifters, football players, boxers, collegiate wrestlers, downhill skiers—and I've come to realize a simple distinction between them and just about everyone else. It became clear to me at the gym, when I witnessed a guy eating rice from a plastic container.

"What the hell are you eating," I asked.

"Rice."

"Rice? At 9 o'clock in the morning?"

"It's part of my program," he replied matter-of-factly. And then he quietly walked away.

There you have it! No need to discuss it. He does what he does, because it needs to be done. Period.

One of my University roommates did hundreds of pushups each night before bed. Another would sit against a wall in an invisible chair, while reading his assigned text.

None of them invented their extreme diets and painful exercises, nor did they particularly enjoy them. But they wanted to change, to be the best they could be during their scenes. And so they sought out advice and then followed that advice, typically training to failure.

There's the distinction. Do you see?

Why do people continue to attend conferences, participate in webinars, and hire consultants? To get the answers? So they can use the information to change their routines, train to failure, and become the best they can be? I don't think so. All of the questions have already been answered, repeatedly. Instead, most people are searching for validation. They're looking for permission to do what they feel like doing, or for someone to motivate them.

The other day I decided to hard-boil some eggs. So I did a quick online search to find a recipe; one that would produce moist yellow yolks (not dry green ones) and, most importantly, eggs that were easy to peel.

I found one.

In fact, I found a lot of them. So, did I follow the instructions to a T? Hell no. I was distracted (by my dog, my smartphone, the latest issue of The Week). And what eventually happened? I bitched at each and every one of those eggs as I struggled to peel them.

I see and hear people bitching all the time, wherever I go. What I rarely see are those same people doing pushups, sitting against a wall, eating rice from plastic containers, and following their recipes to a T.

Willpower is a Choice

Keats wrote, "Do you not see how necessary a world of pains and troubles is to school an intelligence and make it a soul?"

I'm certainly not advocating for a world of pains and troubles, especially not a world ravaged by disease like the one that took twenty-five-year-old John Keats at the height of his genius. But the popular notion that we should try to eliminate, or avoid all potential sources of pain—uncertainty, discomfort, heartache or failure—is another misguided delusion; one driven by Coleridge's desire to stay safe and in control.

I know, we seem to be going around in circles.

I hope this is clear. If your intention, during your short time here on earth, is to avoid pain—and it's your decision—then by all means let Coleridge lead you. He's got it pretty much figured out. And, in case he may have missed something, he'll stay glued to the outpouring of information from the world and advise you when you need to update your beliefs.

But if you're here to live fully, with passion and from the inside out, then let Keats lead you and embrace the loss and pain that comes with the pleasure of that inspired journey.

Are you driven to be an athlete? Then embrace your doubts, and the pain of training and dieting. Do you want to start a business and make a difference? Then welcome the uncertainties, the long hours, and the constant adjustments. Is your passion to perform or to create? Then face your insecurities and accept that you may be rejected, have to work three jobs, live in a cramped apartment, and struggle for years to get your work seen and appreciated (if you're lucky).

This has nothing to do with willpower.

People think willpower is some kind of invisible mental muscle, a mysterious inner strength that we can exercise and which becomes depleted.

It's not.

Quite simply, willpower is a battle. It's a clash of conflicting desires, between those pushed by Coleridge in our happiness-obsessed culture (a big, beautiful boat!) and the ones whispered softly by Keats (more time to practice). Willpower is simply a choice: Now or later. Reality or possibility.

Are people who lack willpower lazy? Do they lack the cognitive power known as self-control? Absolutely not. Their desire for the good feelings of the world are simply greater than their desire for the spirited growth of their inner selves.

Willpower is not a cognitive battle *against* your desires. It's an ongoing struggle *between* them. Give your dreams a fighting chance. Immerse yourself in the surroundings of possibility and replace the superficial, external hype of Coleridge with the impassioned, meaningful pleas of Keats.

You'll find it will make all the difference.

Is Success Happiness?

I read somewhere that success is getting what you want, and happiness is wanting what you get.

It reminded me of Halloween, my favorite childhood holiday. Witches, black cats, and jack-o'-lanterns. Bright eyes, brown paper bags, and old pillow cases. Homemade costumes of gypsies, ghosts, pirates and hobos.

We were uncomfortable, we looked ridiculous, and the candy selection was meager. But we couldn't have cared less, because the night was magical!

It was dark and scary and filled with kids. We were independent and empowered, living in the moment and in it for the experience. We were truly happy.

And then something happened.

Halloween was brought under control by the purveyors of security and the merchants of success. And so we went trick-or-treating when it was "safe;" during daylight hours, in malls, or on more convenient days.

And worse, we started caring and comparing; about our costumes, our candy, and our selfies. We wanted to be successful.

Shannon once asked me, somewhat rhetorically, "Why is success viewed as happiness? Why isn't happiness viewed as success?"

That's a profound and critically important question, and a choice that's all yours. You can *choose* fear, discomfort, and excitement; the thrill of living an incomparable life. Or you can settle for comfort, comparisons, and collecting; the familiar measurements of progress, of success.

"But," you may be wondering. "Isn't that a false distinction? Can't I have both?"

Of course you can. Once you finally realize that happiness is success, and not the other way around.

A Journey to Here

Our society is fixated on the achievement of success and happiness, and the irony is that obsessing over those slippery concepts is what moves us further and further away from them. It's like trying to fall asleep; the harder you try the more anxious and awake you become. So what's the solution?

Relax and trust life.

Bob Dylan proclaimed you're a success if you get up in the morning and go to bed at night and in between you do what you want to do. Gandhi said happiness is when what you think, what you say, and what you do are in harmony. Combine those two ideas and it's pretty simple:

Do what you want to do, and do it in harmony with your inner self.

But that appears to be a very confusing concept, as comically expressed by Charles Schultz's beagle-philosopher Snoopy:

"My life has no purpose, no direction, no aim, no meaning, and yet I'm happy. I can't figure it out. What am I doing right?"

What he's doing right is called negative capability. Success and happiness come from *dropping* your self-important identity, *giving up* the chase for certainty and comfort, and *letting go* of the need to figure everything out.

It's another paradox:

Success is a journey to the place where you already are; the experience of living fully and passionately, right here, right now.

Success and Failure

I know, it's confusing. So, if that's success, then what is failure? Try looking at it like this:

The opposite of dark is light; light makes dark less of what it is. The opposite of hot is cold; adding one to the other diminishes both. And so what's the opposite of success?

The word that probably comes to mind is failure. But that can't be, because failure fosters success. It produces learning, insights and resilience. Success and failure are two sides of the same coin.

It's like exercise and rest.

Rest isn't the opposite of exercise. Rest is what nurtures exercise; it strengthens the body and prepares it for more. Exercise and rest are two sides of the same coin; the fitness coin. Exercise isn't the outcome, fitness is: improved energy, strength and appearance.

Similarly, success isn't an outcome. It's simply one side of a coin: the coin called living. Living the life you are meant to live. And the results are, curiously, the same as fitness:

Energy, strength and appearance.

Energy in body, mind and spirit. Strength of will and character. And appearance, especially to those who matter most. But not a superficial, invented appearance. An inspiring, meaningful one. One built on faith, sacrifice and hard work. One for your children, and your children's children, to learn from and emulate.

So then, what is the opposite of success?

Just like with exercise, the opposite of success is idleness, apathy, a spiritless life of doubt and regret.

Failure is exercise. Success is rest. And a passionate life is a soulful mixture.

Let Go and Be Alive

But it's so much easier said than done, isn't it? Trust me, I know. The desire for certainty and control are overwhelming impulses.

There are boxes of notes stacked up in my office that have been taped closed for years, and I have portable hard drives loaded with data. And I'm pretty sure I'll never access any of it.

Strangely, it makes me feel secure.

The same thing happens with other aspects of our lives. We think that security consists in clinging onto what we have and what we've done. And so we refuse to let go and move forward. Like an old sweater, we clutch what's familiar, what feels right. It helps define and comfort us. It gives us something to depend on. In our minds, it helps us survive. But at what cost?

At the expense of living.

Life is what we do, not what we've done. It's what we create, not what we've accumulated. When you stop clinging, everything changes. Your senses wake up. You see a world rich in possibility; one full of energy, excitement and learning.

Don't cling to survive. Let go and be alive.

You have nothing to lose but your past, and everything to gain—your passion, your significance, your very life. Stop holding on to yesterday's script and improvise.

Because when you stop ad-libbing and innovating, you cease to exist.

Nobody Knows Anything

"Nobody knows anything" is how famed screenwriter William Goldman summed up the entertainment industry in his 1983 memoir. And now, a little more than 30 years later, it appears that everybody knows everything. And we can thank the Internet.

According to research, there's a strange side effect to searching the Internet. When people successfully look something up online, they feel that they have mastered that bit of knowledge. Access to the information makes them feel smarter than they really are.

This is really bad news.

People, in general, already believe that they're better and smarter than average. It's a cognitive bias called illusory superiority. And the Internet is making this bias even more extreme. It's supercharging people's preconceptions and solidifying their false assumptions. And that would be fine if we lived in a utopia. But we don't. We live in an age of rapid change, an age of possibility. And certainty kills possibility; it smothers inspiration and wonder.

I find it so ironic: The Internet creates wonderful possibilities, by opening a space of uncertainty. One where we can learn, connect, create something new and grow. And the Internet takes possibility away by making us feel certain, by shutting down curiosity and learning, and creating a limiting space that isn't interesting, challenging, creative or fulfilling.

Life is, indeed, a paradox. And J.F.K. put it well: "The one unchangeable certainty is that nothing is unchangeable or certain."

And that's because life is not a scripted story, even though it appears that way. Life is improv. We're making it up as we go. But no one will admit it, because it sounds really scary to say it:

Nobody knows anything.

But that should inspire you, because life isn't a linear performance that's heading to some scripted ending. Life is circular. You wake up each day with the opportunity to begin again, to create a new and amazing scene. So be where you feel good and do what brings you joy.

Invented and Fleeting

I once read about some Tibetan monks who were engaged in an age-old ritual. For five days they painstakingly laid millions of grains of colored sand onto a platform. And at the end of their ceremony they planned to sweep it all away, as a meditation on the fleeting nature of life.

But with their mandala about an hour from completion, something fascinating occurred. A toddler wandered onto the platform. The beauty of the monks' elaborate design was simply too much for him to resist.

The happy crowd of onlookers suddenly turned solemn. Even the monks appeared stricken. Hours of work was destroyed in an instant. But what an amazingly symbolic event; a fascinating display of the impermanence of all things. And it was brought to life, fittingly, by an innocent child.

You may be smiling. I am. But you wouldn't have been if it was your mandala, or your spirited child. And that's because we hate it when our plans go awry, or when we look bad to others.

That silly script again.

I've had my own sand mandalas destroyed on many occasions. Some took me years and a lot of money to create, and it used to really bother me.

It also used to irk me when I wasn't taken seriously, or when others considered me childlike, seemingly ignorant to the realities of their world of "how things are done." But I've finally discovered two things:

First, those seemingly crushing setbacks? They released me and compelled me to move to a more exciting and liberating scene.

And, more importantly, those realities people wanted me to accept? Their "how things are done around here?" They weren't some kind of universal truth. In fact, time revealed most of them to be distorted and limiting perspectives; serious, and seriously flawed viewpoints.

So enlighten up.

Life is invented. It's *your* multicolored, three dimensional art. No one else's.

And it's as fleeting as a sand mandala.

Epilogue

Action is character.

— F. Scott Fitzgerald

You're Purpose

Purpose is the new black.
Everyone is busy reframing what they do.
From what to why.
And once it's reimagined, they turn on the storytelling machine.
And wait for attention to blossom.
But this contemporary approach is misguided.
Because purpose isn't conjured up.
It's created.
It isn't a carefully considered and crafted image.
It's a bold statement.
A way of thinking and behaving that grows and evolves and enhances people's lives.
Purpose isn't something we pull out of our ourselves.

It's something we passionately build in.
Out of our spirit, experiences and values.
It's not something that we uncover.
It's an essence that we reveal through our choices and sacrifices.
Purpose means progress.
It's movement towards a more ethical and meaningful way of being.
Purpose creates a new world.
One that compensates for the one we typically experience.
A new world of truth, compassion and excitement.
Purpose is an aspiration.
It's a direction that drives us.
It informs our minds and engages our hearts.
Emerson wrote, "The purpose of life is not to be happy.
It is to be useful, to be honorable, to be compassionate.
To have it make some difference that you have lived and lived well."
The same is true of you and your life.
Are you helpful?

Is what you do enjoyable?

Does it improve people's lives ?

Are you honest, straightforward and trustworthy?

And if you think compassion is a wishy-washy concept, think again.

Compassion is the deep awareness of the suffering of another.

Coupled with the desire to relieve it.

And that's the key to meaning, renewal and growth.

This is not rocket science.

Simply show people that you care.

Get off of your wheel.

And actually give a shit.

The future is not some place that you are going.

It's a reality that you are creating.

Right here, right now!

From your inner voice.

THAT is your real purpose.

And it's up to you to create it.

For your co-workers.

For your community.

For your children.
And for your own soul.

Savor the Squeeze

Alan Watts said, "To come to your senses you have to go out of your mind." For the past three years I've been in and out of my mind, engaged in an exciting and uncomfortable dance with negative capability.

My plunge into uncertainty began with a feeling, a strange whisper telling me to jump! And that voice grew louder and louder, eventually moving me to create a screenplay, this book, a novel, new friendships, a community, and much, much more.

And I had absolutely no idea that any of it would happen.

It happened because I let go of my false sense of security and opened up. I stopped trying to control life with compulsive, conscious efforts and escaped the trap called "me"—my manufactured identity and all of the trappings of that role that kept me attached to my self, like so many invisible Velcro hooks.

Before I tell you a bit about that life-changing plunge, let me answer your nagging questions; the ones your Coleridge mind is simply dying to know:

First of all, no.

As of this writing, the screenplay has still not been picked up and made into a movie. But my venture into the movie industry has been both a fascinating and enlightening experience.

And "the juice?" Was it worth "the squeeze?"

I tossed that expression into this book, because a friend asked me that exact question when I told him about my new scene. It's such an erroneous metaphor. It makes life sound like a tedious chore of accumulation and maintenance, which for many people it is.

And the funny thing is they seem to enjoy it.

Get Off the Wheel

I remember reading about a couple of researchers in the Netherlands who wanted to challenge a prevailing assumption. One that suggests mice run in wheels because they're captive and neurotic, like animals pacing in cages.

So they placed some running wheels in nature and wild mice showed up and ran in them, even in the absence of food rewards. Running in wheels appears to be more than a coping behavior. It may be enjoyable.

Human beings enjoy the wheel, too. The wheel of unconscious, habitual thinking and behavior. The happy trance of the status quo. It makes them feel safe and secure. It gives them the feeling of knowing what to expect.

I used to believe that restless wheel runners were unhappy. But I was wrong. They're as happy as anyone else, perhaps happier. And so they're not going to change very much.

Running in my particular wheel was taking me nowhere and making me sick, when out of that nowhere a voice whispered something ridiculously obvious, "Get off, stupid."

So I did.

A Simple Request

It was another cold, dark New England morning and I was chatting with Shannon at the gym. I had done some advisory work for her and her board, and during a follow up conversation I mentioned my crazy idea for a movie.

"That's a great concept!" she exclaimed. "You should do it." She seemed genuinely excited about the idea.

"I've tried," I replied. "But writing a screenplay is nothing like writing a book. It's a second-by-second description of what someone *sees* on a screen, and I can't conjure visual images in my mind."

She was confused.

"What do you mean, you can't see images in your mind? Aren't you an artist?"

"I can draw and paint what I can see," I explained. "But I don't have a visual memory, so I can't create something realistic from my imagination."

After spending some time discussing my peculiar condition, aphantasia, and struggling to empathize with each other, Shannon revealed that she recalls images in surprising detail. She went on to vividly describe everything in the room behind her and expressed how she has relied on that ability throughout her diverse career.

"And you know," she added. "I'm a movie buff."

"Well, then" I proposed, "Why don't you work with me? We'll create it together."

It was a simple request with an equally simple response, "Okay." And a little over two years later, I found myself traveling to New York City, finished screenplay in hand, to meet with an interested film executive.

Listen Carefully

As time passed, we noticed something quite interesting. Every single person who reviewed the screenplay expressed that they really enjoyed reading it. Having read dozens of screenplays myself, I can assure you that is not a common sentiment. The art form, as a film-making blueprint, doesn't lend itself to an immersive reading experience.

And then Keats whispered, "Well then, turn it into a novel so others can enjoy it."

So we listened (again) and off we went.

I still have no idea what will happen next, and I really don't care. But I am aware of what's happening; around me and inside of me. And that's the ultimate juice of my amazing and exhilarating squeeze.

Similar to Buddhist philosophy, my *I am Keats* journey has helped me view my mind as a sixth sense, in addition to sight, hearing, taste, smell, and touch. My thoughts have become like any other stimuli, a dispassionate source of information.

I never became angry at the smell of sour milk; I knew what it meant and simply discarded it. And now I understand what my thoughts are signaling, and I listen to them without judgment and without comparison. Instead of being a tool for my thinking mind, for Coleridge, Keats and I use Coleridge as *our* tool.

Remember

We're nearing the end of this little book, so now what? What should you do? What should I do?

The Chinese sage Lao Tzu wrote, "A good traveler has no fixed plans and is not intent on arriving." I suppose it doesn't matter what we do. What matters is that we do it. Let's not wait for the perfect opportunity; there is no such thing.

I wanted to open one of my books with "Memento mori (Remember that you must die.)" But my publisher didn't like it. They didn't think it was "positive" enough. So they convinced me to change it to "Carpe diem (Seize the day.)"

And since then, I've often wondered: Why should anyone "seize the day?" Why "pluck the day as it is ripe?" Why not do what most people do and simply suck it up, and patiently wait for better times?

The answer has become painfully clear to me as I watch people I know leave this Earth:

Those better times may never come, because your time must end and you have no idea when. So must mine.

So did Steve Jobs' who said: "Remembering that you are going to die is the best way I know to avoid the trap of thinking that you have something to lose." Yet we seem to remember everything but that reality.

We remember the emails we have to answer. We remember the bills we need to pay. We remember that our car is due for an oil change. We remember because we take comfort in those predictable and manageable activities. We remember because we don't want to lose anything. We remember because we want to avoid unhappiness.

But avoiding unhappiness is not the road to happiness. It's the road to monotony and mediocrity. And while we unthinkingly attend to it, our life suffers.

We forget.

We forget that we're not here to manage affairs, to unthinkingly fit in, play small and feel secure. We're here to stand up and to stand out, to create a scene. It's a self-healing acceptance of our uniqueness, and a soulful lesson to others.

And it's the essential gift, the true legacy, that we provide to our children; a real-life account of how to live, decisively and with full intensity.

So remember.

Remember that you and every person you see will soon be dead. Remember so that you live mindfully. Remember, so that you live with heightened awareness. Remember, so that you don't shrink from being fully alive.

Wait for It

Years ago, my aunt traveled from the south to visit my family. As we neared my home, her eyes became large. She was amazed at the brilliant color of autumn in New England.

Later that day, I decided to take a walk to find her some leaves; vibrant, pristine ones that she could press and take home. So I headed down a well-worn path in the nearby woods; one overflowing with recently fallen leaves.

As I walked along, attentively searching for the perfect leaf, all I could see was decay and various shades of brown. I was dumbfounded. In an area overflowing with foliage, I couldn't find one worthy leaf.

But after about ten minutes of looking, something strange occurred. The forest floor started popping with Crayola color; burnt orange, brick red, lemon yellow. And the leaves seemed to be rising airily from the ground, as if I were wearing 3-D glasses.

It was an extraordinarily rousing and educational experience. My old eyes suddenly became new again, as my brain adjusted to its new environment and to its childlike instructions.

The English biologist John Lubbock wrote, "What we see depends mainly on what we look for."

Where you are and what you attend to conditions what you see. If you look for beauty, truth and love, you'll find it. If you look for facts, reasons and shortcomings, you'll find them. If you want to see new, you have to experience new.

Now it may take time for your old eyes to adjust to a new world, so I'd revise Lubbock's words slightly:

"We *eventually* see what we look for."

So stay focused and be patient. If you're looking with the right intentions and you're looking in the right places, the answers will appear.

I saw what I was looking for, and the spontaneous decision to let go and write a screenplay provided the answers I needed to escape my mind and free my self.

But I still had to "kill my darlings."

That's the advice William Faulkner, among others, imparted to aspiring writers; to cut any aspect of their work that doesn't serve to further it as a whole, even if those elements are precious, self-indulgent ones.

Let go of the comfort of certainty, cut the constraining cords of conformity, kill your darling self-story. The unsettling void of not knowing is the womb of discovery and the birth of a full, intense and meaningful life.

Embrace the paradox.

Stay calm *and* be Keats. Rage, rage against the dying of the light, *and* go gentle into that good night.

...let us not therefore go hurrying about and collecting honey, bee-like buzzing here and there impatiently from a knowledge of what is to be aimed at; but let us open our leaves like a flower and be passive and receptive—budding patiently under the eye of Apollo and taking hints from every noble insect that favours us with a visit—sap will be given us for meat and dew for drink.

— John Keats

Afterword

Books are never finished. They are merely abandoned.

— Oscar Wilde

I may have abandoned my writing between these curious covers, but in no way am I finished with *I am Keats*.

In fact, this is just the beginning.

I've set my true nature free to help others discover their gifts, to provoke their inner spirits to be daring and have faith in providence.

I'm viscerally aware of what that entails.

When I began writing the screenplay and this book, I fought like hell against Coleridge's "irritable reaching after fact and reason." He kept pressing me to be goal-driven and reductive, to break it all down and spell it all out.

I was sympathetic, but I resisted and let Keats lead.

Yet, I have come to realize that these ideas are difficult and somewhat disturbing. Therefore, I've decided to reengage Coleridge to help Keats make sense of these concepts to others, to clarify and codify.

So, if you're interested in diving deeper into the ideas in this book—and working with us to integrate them into your life—please join us at www.iamkeats.com, where our aim is straightforward:

To set you free!

About the Author

Tom Asacker is often described as a creative force, albeit a wayward one. He is an artist, writer, inventor, and philosopher. He writes, teaches, and speaks about radically new practices and ideas for success in times of uncertainty and change.

For Further Information, Please Visit our Website at:

www.iamkeats.com

41117654R00088

Made in the USA
Middletown, DE
04 March 2017